A Trail in th

Contents

Written by Suzannah Ditchburn

Collins

Spot things on your trail

The sun is bright in spring. It allows us to spot interesting animals and trees.

green woodpecker

chaffinch

tree creeper

The brook

You can splash in the brook.
You might spot a stoat.

a frog croaking

brook

Clamber up trees.

Do not disturb nests.

black poplar

oak tree

5

Tracking animals

Track animal footprints.

Do not frighten animals.

squirrel tracks

snail trail

6

stoat tracks

It is important to avoid spoiling animal trails.

Animals can hunt by smelling animal trails.

What is that?

You might spot flowers in spring.

cowslip

You might spot an animal den on the trail.

treetop squirrel den

rabbit den

fox den

Put up a den!

Start your den by collecting sticks.

Do not spoil the woods.

Construct a wooden tent on your trail. Add green moss for a rainproof roof.

crisscross sticks

Construct a scrapbook with your trail snapshots!

fox den

squirrel tracks

It is interesting and fun on a woodland trail!

treetop den

tree creeper

A woodland trail

After reading

Letters and Sounds: Phase 4

Word count: 167

Focus on adjacent consonants with long vowel phonemes, e.g. /t/ /r/ /ai/ /l/

Common exception words: your, the, by, what, put, do, to, you

Curriculum links: Plants; Animals, including humans; Seasonal changes

National Curriculum learning objectives: Reading/word reading: apply phonic knowledge and skills as the route to decode words, read accurately by blending sounds in unfamiliar words containing GPCs that have been taught, read other words of more than one syllable that contain taught GPCs, read aloud accurately books that are consistent with their developing phonic knowledge, re-read books to build up their fluency and confidence in word reading; Reading/comprehension: link what they have read or hear read to their own experiences, discuss word meanings, discuss the significance of the title and events

Developing fluency

- Your child may enjoy hearing you read the book.
- Discuss the layout of the text and features of the non-fiction text such as headings, labels and captions with your child. Think about how these help the reader to navigate the text.
- Look at the use of punctuation marks such as question marks and exclamation marks and discuss how these affect the expression used when reading aloud. Practise together with some examples from the books.

Phonic practice

- Model reading words with adjacent consonants and long vowel sounds. Take the word **brook**. Say each of the sounds quickly and clearly, b/r/oo/k. Then blend the sounds together. Ask your child to do the same.
- Now ask your child to sound out and blend the following words:
  croak   tree   bright   snail

Extending vocabulary

- Ask your child:
  o What does the word "clamber" mean? (e.g. *to climb*)
  o How many different words can you think of that mean clamber? (e.g. *climb, scramble, scale, mount, crawl*)
  o Think of a sentence using the word "clamber". (e.g. *The cat clambered over the garden fence.*)